A Book of Friendship

Prayers, Poems and Scriptures

Regina Press
New York

First published in Great Britain in 1994 by
KEVIN MAYHEW LTD
Rattlesden
Bury St Edmunds
Suffolk IP30 OSZ

*Dedicated to the memory of our dear friend,
Harry Costello. We will miss you, and always treasure
the memories of our times together.*

GEORGE AND ROBERT

ISBN 088271 499 6

1996 The Regina Press

Printed in Belgium

CONTENTS

FRIENDSHIP

A friend is like a tower strong;
a friend is like the joyous song
that helps us on our way.

When golden ties of friendship bind
the heart to heart, the mind to mind
how fortunate are we!

For friendship is a noble thing;
it soars past death on angel's wing
into eternity.

God blesses friendship's holy bond
both here and in the great beyond:
a benefit unpriced.

Then may we know that wondrous joy,
that precious ore without alloy;
a friendship based on Christ.

Friendships begun in this world
will be taken up again,
never to be broken off.

FRANCIS DE SALES

Take Courage!

I can't change what you're going through,
I have no words to make a difference,
no answers or solutions
to make things easier for you.

But if it helps in any way
I want to say I care.

Please know that even when you're lonely
you're not alone.

I'll be here,
supporting you with all my thoughts,
cheering for you with all my strength,
praying for you with all my heart.

For whatever you need,
for as long as it takes –

Lean on my love.

LOVE

Love is patient and kind;
it is not jealous or conceited or proud.
Love is not ill-mannered
or selfish or irritable;
Love does not keep a record of wrongs;
Love is not happy with evil
but is happy with the truth.
Love never gives up;
and its faith, hope and patience
never fail.

I CORINTHIANS 13:4-7

A friendship
which makes the least noise
is often
the most useful.

How Many Times?

Peter asked Jesus,
'If someone offends me,
how often should I forgive;
say, seven times?'
Jesus answered,
'Not merely seven times,
I tell you,
but seventy times seven.'

MATTHEW 18:21-22

❧

True friendship
ought never to conceal
what it thinks.

ST JEROME

To Know Someone

To know someone here or there
with whom you feel
there is understanding
in spite of differences
or thoughts unexpressed –
that can make of this earth
a garden.

A friend is the one
who comes in
when the whole world
has gone out.

The fruit of the Spirit is love,
joy, peace, gentleness, goodness,
faith, meekness, temperance.

GALATIANS 5:22-23

May God,
who understands each need,
who listens to every prayer,
bless you and keep you
in his loving, tender care.

I Asked Jesus

I asked Jesus,
'How much do
you love me?'
'This much,'
he answered, and
he stretched out
his arms and died.

May your love enfold me,
may your peace surround me,
may your light touch me.

GOD'S MOST
PRECIOUS GIFT

There's a miracle
called Friendship
that dwells within the heart
and you don't know
how it happens
or when it gets its start.
But the happiness
it brings to you
always gives a special lift
and you realise
that friendship
is God's most precious gift.

Hold a true friend
with both your hands.

21

I Said a Prayer

I said a prayer for you today
and know God must have heard –
I felt the answer in my heart
although he spoke no word!
I didn't ask for wealth or fame
(I knew you wouldn't mind) –
I asked him to send treasures
of a far more lasting kind!

I asked that he'd be near you
at the start of each new day
to grant you health and blessings
and friends to share your way!
I asked for happiness for you
in all things great and small –
but it was for his loving care
I prayed the most of all!

WHEN YOU'RE LONELY

When you're lonely,
I wish you love.

When you're down,
I wish you joy.

When you're troubled,
I wish you peace.

When things are complicated,
I wish you simple beauty.

When things look empty
I wish you hope.

DEEP PEACE

Deep peace of the Running Wave to you.
Deep peace of the Flowing Air to you.
Deep peace of the Quiet Earth to you.
Deep peace of the Shining Stars to you.
Deep peace of the Son of Peace to you.

CELTIC BENEDICTION

LIFE'S LESSONS

After a while
you learn the difference
between holding a hand
and chaining a soul.
You learn that love isn't leaning,
but lending support.
You begin to accept your defeats
with the grace of an adult,
not the grief of a child.

You decide to build
your roads on today,
for tomorrow's ground
is too uncertain.
You help someone plant a garden
instead of waiting
for someone to bring you flowers.
You learn that God has given you
the strength to endure,
and that you really do have worth.

T.F.Collier
1885

A Blessing

May the Lord bless you
and take care of you;

May the Lord be kind
and gracious to you;

May the Lord look on you with favour
and give you peace.

Numbers 6:22-27

ACKNOWLEDGEMENTS

The publishers wish to express their gratitude to Fine Art Photographic Library Ltd., London, and the Galleries listed below, for permission to reproduce the pictures in this book:

Front Cover THE BASKET OF FLOWERS by William Peter Watson (d. 1932).
Gavin Graham Gallery.

Page 4 A WALLED GARDEN by John Parker (1839-1915).
Bourne Gallery.

Pages 6 & 7 OUT OF SCHOOL by Myles Birket Foster (1825-1899).
Polak Gallery, London SW1.

Page 8 THE GARDEN PATH by James Matthews.
City Wall Gallery.

Page 11 CHILDREN ON A DONKEY by Myles Birket Foster (1825-1899)

Page 12 THE TIN WHISTLE by Charles Edward Wilson (d. 1941).
Hinson Fine Paintings.

Page 14 THE GARDEN AT GOLDEN FIELD, LIPHOOK by Juliet N. Williams (early 20c).
Cooper Fine Arts, London.

Pages 16 & 17 MAIDEN VOYAGE by Myles Birket Foster (1825-1899).

Page 18 A PICNIC IN THE WOODS by Edgar Barclay (1842-1913).
Caelt Gallery.

Page 21 SPRING DECORATIONS by Agnes Gardner King (d. 1929).

Page 22 RHODODENDRONS AND BUTTERFLIES by Marion Ellis Rowan (1842-1922).
Gavin Graham Gallery.

Pages 24 & 25 THE HERBACIOUS BORDER by Patrick William Adam (1854-1930).
Julian Simon Gallery.

Page 26 A SWING OF LOVE by William Strutt (1827-1915).
Anthony Mitchell Fine Paintings.

Page 29 STILL LIFE OF PANSIES AND PELARGONIUMS by Thomas Frederick Collier (19c.)
Private Collection.

Page 30 A FOREST GLADE IN SPRINGTIME by Johannes Boesen (1847-1916).